Piano/Vocal/Chords

80 YEARS OF POPULAR MUSIC

THE SIXTIES

Project Manager: CAROL CUELLAR
Copy Editors: NADINE DEMARCO & DONNA SALZBURG
Cover Design: HEADLINE PUBLICITY LIMITED
Book Art Layout: LISA GREENE MANE
Text Research: CAROL CUELLAR & DAVID C. OLSEN

1960

The sixties soared into sight with John F. Kennedy being too young to be elected President and Stan Musial being too old to keep running the bases. Both got where they were going. It was the year of the beatniks and of lunch counter sit-ins in the South. It was the year that Gary Power's U-2 was shot down over Russia. The Yankees won the pennant, Hugh Hefner chose to open his new Playboy Club in Chicago, and Chubby Checker performed "The Twist" on American television for the first time on Dick Clark's "American Bandstand." *The Apartment* won the Oscar and *To Kill a Mockingbird* was the year's top book.

1961

The space race was heating up with the Russians putting two men in orbit while the U.S. had its first sub-orbital flights. While things were heating up in outer space, the deep freeze was blowing colder with headlines of the Berlin Wall and the Bay of Pigs. JFK also gave us the Peace Corps while the Peppermint Lounge in New York gave us "The Twist." People were being hijacked to Cuba, and we watched busloads of freedom riders in the Deep South. Roger Maris was the top athlete of the year, breaking Babe Ruth's 1927 single-season home run mark. The top new book was *The Carpetbaggers* (along with the James Bond books) and *Camelot* was Broadway's best.

1962

John Glenn orbited the earth three times in less than five hours to become the first American to orbit the planet. Back on earth, JFK had his hands full with civil rights in the South, the steel industry in the North, and missiles in Cuba. It was the year when the Seattle World's Fair opened; Telstar was sent into orbit, opening the way to live transoceanic TV broadcasts; and a 114-day newspaper strike closed down seven New York City newspapers. History's worst plane disaster occurred in Paris, killing 130 Americans. On the lighter side, Elizabeth Taylor and Richard Burton were filming *Cleopatra*, and Richard Rodgers had his first musical opening without the aid of his long-time co-writer Oscar Hammerstein II.

1963

More and more racial unrest and freedom walks in the South, no more Bible reading in the schools as dictated by the highest court in the land, the British version of the Great Train Robbery, and the death of a Pope—we were going along nicely until that fated weekend when we learned the names of Oswald and Ruby, and JFK was dead. Suddenly, we had a new President. Chess Records' labelmates Chuck Berry and Bo Diddley were among the black R&B stars with records on the U.S. charts.

1964

The Supremes topped the U.S. singles chart with "Where Did Our Love Go," the first of 12 U.S. chart-toppers before Diana Ross left the group in late 1969. It was the year of topless bathing suits and discotheques and a boxer named Cassius Clay. But while the forties had Sinatra and the fifties had Presley, the year of 1964 could be best remembered for the four mop-topped lads from Liverpool who would dominate the music scene for the next ten years: The Beatles had arrived. Their electronic sounds and shrill vocals would set the pattern of our modern music for a generation. It was also a banner year for Broadway: *Hello, Dolly; Funny Girl;* and *Fiddler on the Roof* all produced box office records and spin-off hit songs.

1965

Draft cards were being burned and people were marching on Washington. There were peace demonstrations and picket lines and five days of rioting in Watts. The Northeast had its 12-hour "Big Blackout" and men walked in space. LBJ unveiled his Great Society, just in time to ensure his 61 percent majority victory at the polls that November. We remembered, if only for a moment, the second world war with the passing of Winston Churchill. The American Black Muslim leader, Malcolm X, was shot dead while addressing a meeting in New York. A Beatles concert drew 56,000 fans to Shea Stadium, New York, and created a new outdoor audience record. Truman Capote published *In Cold Blood*, and Julie Andrews was our biggest box office star with *Mary Poppins* and *The Sound of Music*.

1966

Rioting in the streets of Chicago and Cleveland along with Stokely Carmichael's cry of "Black Power" reminded us that it was a long, hot summer. There was mass murder in Chicago and a sniper in Texas, accounting for a total of 22 dead and 45 wounded. There, too, was Vietnam, which looked more and more like a no-win situation. Yet there were plenty of lighter happenings—miniskirts, the marriage of the President's daughter, and movies like *Doctor Zhivago* and TV shows like "Batman."

1967

It was a time for flower children, hippies, and Haight-Ashbury. We saw Elvis get married (at the age of 32) and Shirley Temple run for Congress. It was the year of the first Super Bowl and the first heart transplant. Jack Ruby was dead, Cassius Clay (not Mohammed Ali) was stripped of his boxing crown, the Six-Day War was fought in the Middle East, and we increased our effort in Vietnam. Aretha Franklin made her U.K. chart debut with the cover of Otis Redding's classic, "Respect." *Rolling Stone* magazine, the first rock 'n' roll periodical in the U.S., made its debut. This year also brought us *The Death of a President* and *Bonnie and Clyde*.

1968

History was made in this year like no other since World War II. Martin Luther King and Robert Kennedy were assassinated, LBJ said "no" to a second term, there was the Pueblo Incident, and Richard Nixon was elected President. Too, we saw the start of the Paris peace talks, Americans orbit the moon, and Jackie Kennedy's marriage to Aristotle Onassis. It was the year of "Laugh-In" and Tiny Tim, of Nehru suits and *The Graduate*.

1969

The world saw the first man walk on the moon on TV and heard the words, "That's one small step for man, one giant leap for mankind." Four months later, it would happen again, and the American's could proudly claim that we won the race into space. But there were even more surprises: The underdog New York Jets won the Super Bowl and the New York Mets won the World Series. Jim Morrison's Miami mayhem at a Doors concert ended with his arrest for lewd and lascivious behavior. Beatle Paul McCartney married American Linda Eastman, a descendent of George Eastman, the inventor of the Kodak camera. The Beach Boys, one of the most successful acts ever signed to Capitol Records, started legal proceedings against the company. An estimated 300,000 people were expected to attend a three-day Woodstock Music and Art Fair in New York with performers including Jimi Hendrix, Joan Baez, Ravi Shanker, Janis Joplin, The Who, and Jefferson Airplane. Broadway opened our eyes (and shocked many) with *Oh! Calcutta* and *Hair*.

CONTENTS

YOU DON'T KNOW LIKE I KNOW

Words and Music by
ISAAC HAYES
and DAVE PORTER

Chorus:
You don't know like I know what that wom-an has done for me.

In the morn-ing she's my wa-ter, in the

eve-ning she's my cup of tea. Man a-lone has not lived,

You Don't Know Like I Know - 4 - 1

BABY, IT'S YOU

Words and Music by
BURT BACHARACH, MACK DAVID
and BARNEY WILLIAMS

BAD MOON RISING

Words and Music by
J.C. FOGERTY

BARBARA ANN

Bright Rock Tempo

Words and Music by
FRED FASSERT

Barbara Ann - 2 - 1

THE BEAT GOES ON

Words and Music by
SONNY BONO

The Beat Goes On,—

The Beat Goes On.

Drums keep pound-ing rhyth-m to the brain,———— La da da da

di.———— La da da da da.————

BIG BAD JOHN

Words and Music by
JIMMY DEAN

Big Bad John - 2 - 1

Recitation:

Verse 1:
Every morning at the mine you could see him arrive,
He stood six-foot-six and weighed two-forty-five.
Kind of broad at the shoulder and narrow at the hip,
And everybody knew you didn't give no lip to Big John!
(Refrain)

Verse 2:
Nobody seemed to know where John called home,
He just drifted into town and stayed all alone.
He didn't say much, a-kinda quiet and shy,
And if you spoke at all, you just said, "Hi" to Big John!
Somebody said he came from New Orleans,
Where he got in a fight over a Cajun queen.
And a crashing blow from a huge right hand
Sent a Louisiana fellow to the promised land. Big John!
(Refrain)

Verse 3:
Then came the day at the bottom of the mine
When a timber cracked and the men started crying.
Miners were praying and hearts beat fast,
And everybody thought that they'd breathed their last 'cept John.
Through the dust and the smoke of this man-made hell
Walked a giant of a man that the miners knew well.
Grabbed a sagging timber and gave out with a groan,
And, like a giant oak tree, just stood there alone. Big John!
(Refrain)

Verse 4:
And with all of his strength, he gave a mighty shove;
Then a miner yelled out, "There's a light up above!"
And twenty men scrambled from a would-be grave,
And now there's only one left down there to save; Big John!
With jacks and timbers they started back down
Then came that rumble way down in the ground,
And smoke and gas belched out of that mine,
Everybody knew it was the end of the line for Big John!
(Refrain)

Verse 5:
Now they never re-opened that worthless pit,
They just placed a marble stand in front of it;
These few words are written on that stand:
"At the bottom of this mine lies a big, big man; Big John!"
(Refrain)

BIRD DOG

Words and Music by
BOUDLEAUX BRYANT

Bird Dog - 3 - 1

Verse 2:

Johnny sings a love song. (Like a bird)
He sings the sweetest love song. (You ever heard)
But when he sings to my gal. (What a howl)
To me he's just a wolf dog. (On the prowl)
Johnny wants to fly away and puppy love my baby.
(He's a bird dog.) *(To Chorus:)*

Verse 3:

Johnny kissed the teacher. (He's a bird)
He tiptoed up to reach her. (He's a bird)
Well, he's the teacher's pet now. (He's a dog)
What he wants he can get now. (What a dog)
He even made the teacher let him sit next to my baby.
(He's a bird dog.) *(To Chorus:)*

BORN UNDER A BAD SIGN

Words and Music by
WILLIAM BELL and
BOOKER T. JONES

Born Under a Bad Sign - 3 - 1

Born Under a Bad Sign - 3 - 3

BLUE MOON

Lyrics by
LORENZ HART

Music by
RICHARD RODGERS

BREAD AND BUTTER

Words and Music by
JAY TURNBOW and LARRY PARKS

Bread and Butter - 2 - 1

CHORUS

He likes BREAD AND BUT-TER   He likes toast and jam

That's what his ba - by feeds him   He's her lov - in'

man   He's her lov - in' man

2nd Verse
She don't cook mashed potatoes
Don't cook T-bone steak
Don't feed me peanut butter
She knows that I can't take

3rd Verse
Got home early one mornin'
Much to my surprise
She was eatin' chicken and dumplins
With some other guy

2nd Chorus
No more BREAD AND BUTTER
No more toast and jam
He found his baby eatin'
With some other man

4th Verse
No more BREAD AND BUTTER
No more toast and jam
I found my baby eatin'
With some other man

Bread and Butter - 2 - 2

CALIFORNIA GIRLS

Words and Music by
BRIAN WILSON

Moderately

1. Well,

East coast girls are hip, I real-ly dig those styles they
West coast has the sun-shine, and the girls all get so

wear._____ And the south-ern girls with the
tanned._____ I dig a French bi-kini with on a

way they talk, they knock me out when I'm down there._____
wild island coast_____ by a palm tree in the sand.

California Girls - 3 - 1

The mid-west far-mers' daugh-ters real-ly
I been all 'round this great big world and I've

make you feel al - right.___ And the north-ern girls with the
seen all kinds of girls.___ But I could-n't wait to get

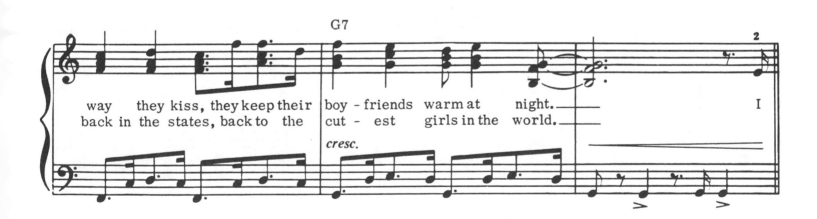

way they kiss, they keep their boy-friends warm at night.___ I
back in the states, back to the cut-est girls in the world.___

Chorus:

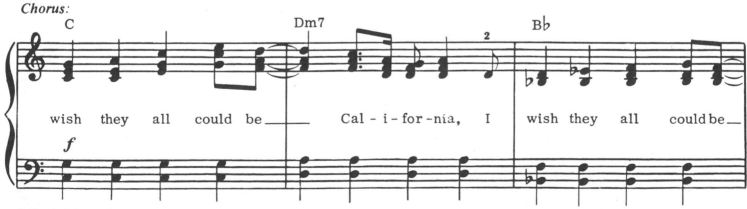

wish they all could be___ Cal-i-for-nia, I wish they all could be___

California Girls - 3 - 2

CLASSICAL GAS

Music by
MASON WILLIAMS

Classical Gas - 3 - 1

Classical Gas - 3 - 2

D.S. al ◆ Coda
(taking 2nd time bar)

Coda

rall

Classical Gas - 3 - 3

CATHY'S CLOWN

Words and Music by
DON EVERLY and
PHIL EVERLY

Cathy's Clown - 2 - 1

2nd Verse

When you see me shed a tear
And you know that it's sincere
Don't you think it's kind of sad
That you're treating me so bad
Or don't you even care?

CRIMSON AND CLOVER

Words and Music by
TOMMY JAMES and PETER LUCIA

Crimson and Clover - 2 - 1

Crimson and Clover - 2 - 2

CRYING

Words and Music by
ROY ORBISON and JOE MELSON

Crying - 2 - 1

2nd Chorus:
I thought that I was over you
But it's true, so true
I love you even more than I did before
But darling, what can I do?
For you don't love me and I'll always be
CRYING over you, CRYING over you
Yes, now you're gone and from this moment on
I'll be CRYING, CRYING, CRYING, CRYING
Yeah, CRYING, CRYING over you

DO WAH DIDDY DIDDY

Words and Music by
JEFF BARRY and ELLIE GREENWICH

Do Wah Diddy Diddy - 3 - 1

(Sittin' On)
THE DOCK OF THE BAY

Words and Music by
OTIS REDDING and
STEVE CROPPER

Sit-tin' in the morn - ing sun, _____ I'll be sit-tin' till the eve-nin' _ come, _
left _ my _ home _ in Geor - gia, head - ed for the Fris - co _ Bay. _
Sit - tin' here rest-in' my bones _____ and this lone - li-ness won't leave me a-lone. _

_ watch - in' the ships _ roll in, _____ then I
_ I have _____ noth - ing to live _____ for, look like
_ Two thou-sand miles _ I roam _____ just to

48

The Dock of the Bay - 3 - 3

DO YOU WANT TO KNOW A SECRET?

Words and Music by
JOHN LENNON and
PAUL McCARTNEY

Do You Want to Know a Secret? - 2 - 1

DOWN IN THE BOONDOCKS

Words and Music by
JOE SOUTH

Down in the Boondocks - 2 - 1

Down in the Boondocks - 2 - 2

ELUSIVE BUTTERFLY

Words and Music by
BOB LIND

Elusive Butterfly - 2 - 1

EVERYBODY'S TALKIN' (ECHOES)

Words and Music by
FRED NEIL

Everybody's Talkin' (Echoes) - 2 - 1

FUN, FUN, FUN

Words and Music by
BRIAN WILSON and
MIKE LOVE

Fun, Fun, Fun - 4 - 1

A7
A7+
brar - y like she told her "Old man" now.
And with her
like a Ro - man char - i - ot race now.
A lot - ta
D
G
ra - di - o blast - in', goes cruis - in' just as fast as she can now.
guys try to catch her, but she leads 'em on a wild goose chase now.
D
F#m
G
A7
And she'll have fun, fun, fun, till her dad - dy takes the T - Bird a - way.
D
G
1. D
A7
A7+
2. D
A7
2. Well, the

GOOD VIBRATIONS

Words and Music by
BRIAN WILSON and
MIKE LOVE

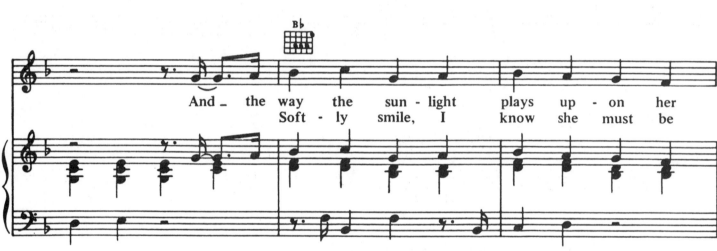

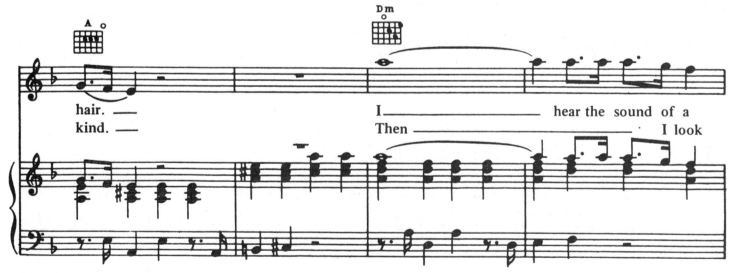

Good Vibrations - 3 - 1

GREEN ONIONS

Music by
BOOKER T. JONES, STEVE CROPPER,
LEWIS STEINBERG and AL JACKSON, JR.

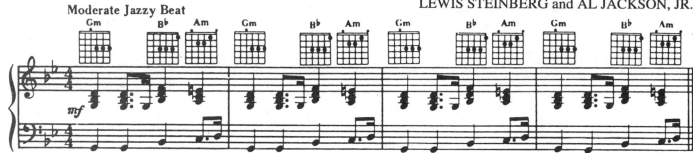

Green Onions - 3 - 1

Green Onions - 3 - 3

GREEN TAMBOURINE

Words and Music by
SHELLEY PINZ and
PAUL LEKA

Drop your sil - ver in my tam-bou -rine;
Watch the jin - gle jan - gle start to shine,
Drop a dime be -fore I walk a - way.

Help a poor man build a pret - ty
Re - flec -tions of the mu - sic that is
An - y song you want I'll glad -ly

dream.
mine.
play.

Give me pen - nies, I'll take an - y - thing.
When you toss a coin you'll hear it sing.
Mon - ey feeds my mu - sic ma - chine.

Now

Green Tambourine - 2 - 1

lis – ten while I play _____ my green tam – bou –

rine. _____

rine. _____

rine. _____

Now lis – ten and I'll play. _____

SHE LOVES YOU

Words and Music by
JOHN LENNON and
PAUL McCARTNEY

She Loves You - 3 - 1

HELP ME RHONDA

Words and Music by
BRIAN WILSON

help me, Rhon-da, Help me get her out of my heart._

CHORUS

Help me, Rhon - da! Help, Help me, Rhon - da! Help me, Rhon - da!

Help, Help me, Rhon - da! Help me, Rhon - da! Help, Help me, Rhon - da!

Help me, Rhon - da! Help, Help me, Rhon - da! Help me, Rhon - da!

Help Me Rhonda - 3 - 2

Help, Help me, Rhon - da! Help me, Rhon - da! Help, Help me, Rhon - da!

Help me, Rhon-da! Yeah, get her out of my heart.__ 2. She was

Help me, Rhon - da!

Repeat and fade out

Help, Help me, Rhon - da! Help me, Rhon - da! Help, Help me, Rhon - da!

Help Me Rhonda - 3 - 3

HEY! PAULA

Words and Music by
RAY HILDERBRAND

(Your Love Has Lifted Me)
HIGHER AND HIGHER

Words and Music by
GARY JACKSON, CARL SMITH
and RAYNARD MINER

Higher and Higher - 3 - 1

HOLD ON! I'M COMING

Words and Music by
ISAAC HAYES and
DAVID PORTER

Moderately, with a strong beat

Don't you ev-er feel sad, ___ lean on me when times ___ ___ are bad. ___ When the day ___ comes and you're down ___ in a riv-er of trou-ble and I got to drown, just hold on, I'm com-in'. Hold

Hold On! I'm Coming - 3 - 1

Hold On! I'm Coming - 3 - 2

THE HOUSE OF THE RISING SUN

Words and Music by
ALAN PRICE

The House of the Rising Sun - 3 - 1

The House of the Rising Sun - 3 - 3

I GOT YOU BABE

Words and Music by
SONNY BONO

Slow rock tempo

I Got You Babe - 5 - 1

I Got You Babe - 5 - 2

I SAW HER STANDING THERE

Words and Music by
JOHN LENNON and
PAUL McCARTNEY

I Saw Her Standing There - 3 - 3

I KNEW YOU WHEN

Words and Music by
JOE SOUTH

Moderately

Yeah! Yeah! Yeah! Yeah! Yeah! Yeah!

Chorus:

Yeah! Yeah, ____ yeah. ____ I knew you when you were

lone - ly. I knew you

I Knew You When - 4 - 1

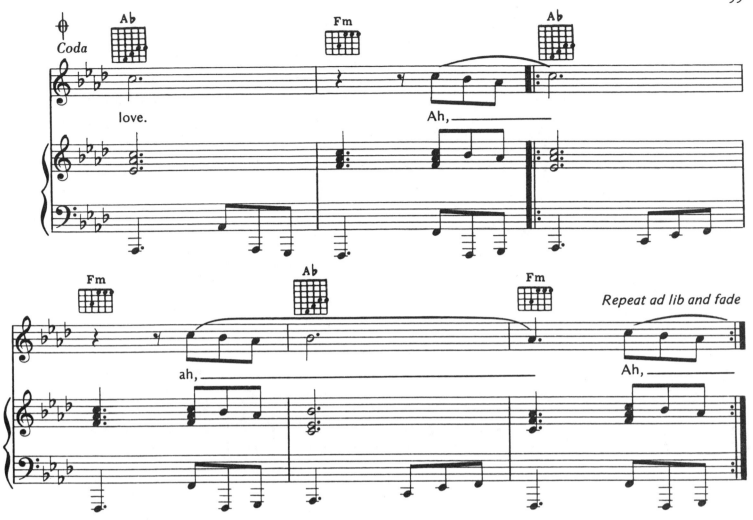

Verse 2:
I knew you when
We used to have a lot of fun,
But someone came and offered more;
Now I'm the lonely one.
I knew you when
I was just a scared little girl.
I used to be your only love
Before you came up in the world.

I Knew You When - 4 - 4

I SAY A LITTLE PRAYER

Words by
HAL DAVID

Music by
BURT BACHARACH

I Say a Little Prayer - 4 - 1

I Say a Little Prayer - 4 - 2

how I'll love you. To-geth-er, to-geth-er, that's how it must be. To

live with-out you would on-ly mean heart-break for me.

1. Smoothly

(Tacet)

2. Smoothly

(Tacet)

me. My dar-ling, be-lieve me,

for me there is no one but

IT'S GOOD NEWS WEEK

Words and Music by
KENNETH KING

It's Good News Week - 2 - 2

IN THE MIDNIGHT HOUR

Words by
WILSON PICKETT

Music by
STEVE CROPPER

In the Midnight Hour - 3 - 1

hold you, and do all the things I told you in the mid-night

hour. Yes, I am, oh yes, I am.

I'm gon-na wait til stars come out _____ and see that

twin-kle in your eyes, I'm gon-na wait til the mid-night

In the Midnight Hour - 3 - 3

KNOCK ON WOOD

Words and Music by
EDDIE FLOYD and
STEVE CROPPER

Knock on Wood - 3 - 1

The way you love me is fright - nin'; Ev - 'ry - bod - y

knock knock knock knock on wood. _____ I'm not sup - er -

wood. _____ Ev - 'ry - bod - y knock knock.

Ev - 'ry - bod - y knock knock.

Repeat and fade

Knock on Wood - 3 - 3

INDIAN RESERVATION
(The Lament of the Cherokee Reservation Indian)

Words and Music by
JOHN D. LOUDERMILK

Indian Reservation - 4 - 1

Indian Reservation - 4 - 2

tie ... I'm still a red man deep in - side

But may - be some - day when they've

learned ... Cher - o - kee Na - tion will re - turn _____

Indian Reservation - 4 - 4

I'VE BEEN LOVING YOU TOO LONG

Words and Music by
OTIS REDDING and
JERRY BUTLER

I've Been Loving You Too Long - 2 - 1

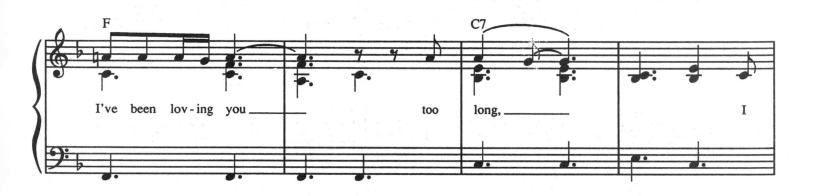

Verse 2:
With you, my life has been so wonderful;
I can't stop now.
You are tired
And your love is growing cold,
My love is growing stronger
As our affair grows old.

JOHNNY ANGEL

Words by
LYN DUDDY

Music by
LEE POCKRISS

CHORUS

John - ny An - gel How I love him, He's got some-thing that I can't re-sist. But he does - n't ev - en know that I ____ ex - ist. ____ John - ny An - gel How I want him, How I tin - gle when he pass - es by. ____ Ev - 'ry - time he says, "Hel - lo" my heart be - gins to fly. ____ I'm in

Johnny Angel - 2 - 1

LET'S GET TOGETHER

By
CHET POWERS

1. Love is but the song we sing, and fear's the way we
2. Some will come and some will go, and we shall sure - ly
3. If you heard the song I sing, you must un - der-

Let's Get Together - 3 - 1

MOCKINGBIRD

Words and Music by
INEZ FOXX and CHARLIE FOXX
Additional Lyrics by JAMES TAYLOR

Moderate beat

Ev-er-y-bod-y have you heard? He's gon-na buy__ me a mock-ing-bird,__

And if that mock-ing-bird__ won't sing,__ he's gon-na buy__

__ me a dia-mond ring,__ And if that dia-mond ring won't shine,__

Mockingbird - 3 - 1

Well, now, everybody have you heard?
She's gonna buy me a mocking bird
If that mocking bird don't sing,
She's gonna buy me a diamond ring.
And if that diamond ring won't shine
Guess it surely break this poor heart of mine,
And that's the reason why I keep on tellin' everybody sayin'
No, no, no, no, no, no, no, no.

Listen now and understand
She's gonna find me some peace of mind.
And if that peace of mind won't stay,
I'm gonna get myself a better way
I might rise above, I might go below,
Ride with the tide and go with the flow,
And that's the reason why I keep on shouting in your ears, y'all
No, no, no, no, no, no, now, now, baby.

Mockingbird - 3 - 3

LITTLE DEUCE COUPE

Words by
ROGER CHRISTIAN

Music by
BRIAN WILSON

Medium Rock beat

Tacet

Well, I'm not brag-gin', babe, so don't put me down,_ but
lit - tle deuce coupe with a flat-head mill,_ but she'll

I've got the fast-est set of wheels in town._ When some-thing pulls up to me, it
walk a Thun-der-bird like it's stand-in' still._ She's port-ed and re-lieved, and she's

Little Deuce Coupe - 4 - 1

Little Deuce Coupe - 4 - 4

MOTHER-IN-LAW

Words and Music by
ALAIN TOUSSAINT

Mother-In-Law - 2 - 2

MR. PITIFUL

Words and Music by
OTIS REDDING &
STEVE CROPPER

Mr. Pitiful - 3 - 1

to un-der-stand___ now, what makes a man___ feel___ so blue.___

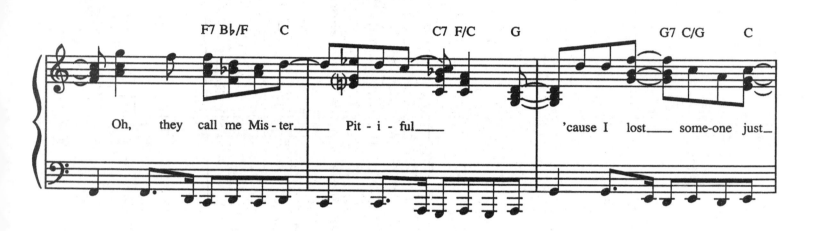

Oh, they call me Mis-ter___ Pit-i-ful___ 'cause I lost___ some-one just___

To Coda ⊕ |1.

___ like you.___   2. They call___ me Mis-ter___

D.S. 𝄋 ||2.

Bridge:

Mr. Pitiful - 3 - 2

Verse 2:
They call me Mr. Pitiful; yes, everybody knows, now.
They call me Mr. Pitiful most every place I go.
But nobody seems to understand, now, what makes a man sing such a sad song,
When he lost everything, when he lost everything he had.
(To Bridge:)

PRIVATE NUMBER

Words and Music by
BOOKER T. JONES
and WILLIAM BELL

Private Number - 3 - 1

I've been lov-ing you _____ and you've been lov-ing me _____ so
I had the num-ber changed, _____ but I'm not act-ing strange. _____ Wel - come

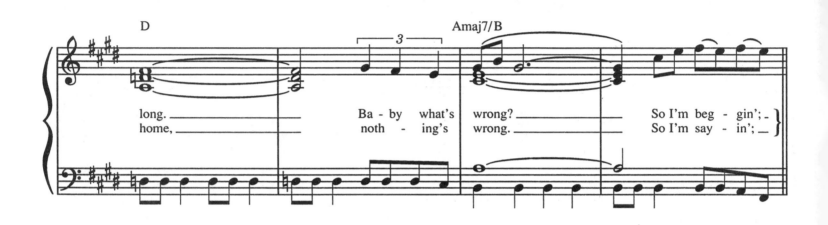

long. _____ Ba - by what's wrong? _____ So I'm beg - gin'; __
home, _____ noth - ing's wrong. _____ So I'm say - in'; __

Chorus:

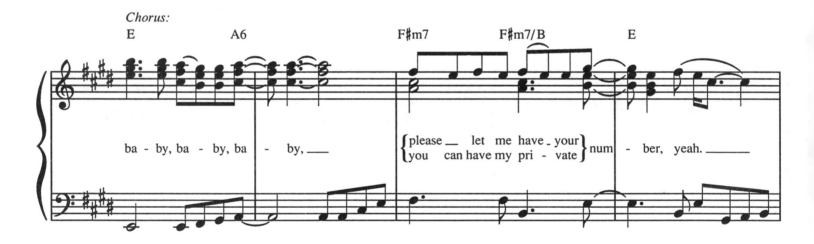

ba - by, ba - by, ba - by, ___ { please ___ let me have _ your } num - ber, yeah. _____
{ you can have my pri - vate }

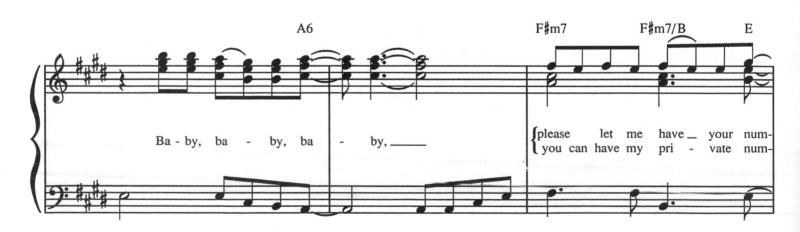

Ba - by, ba - by, ba - by, _____ { please let me have _ your num- }
{ you can have my pri - vate num- }

Private Number - 3 - 2

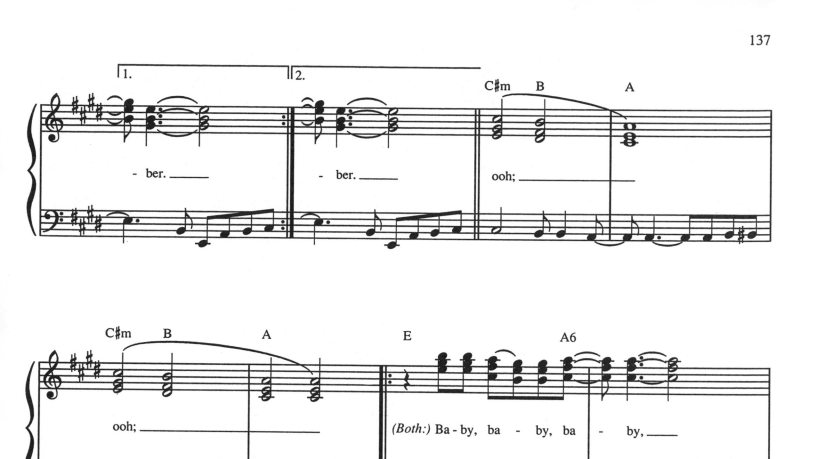

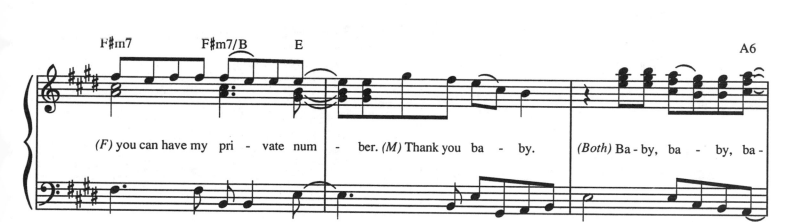

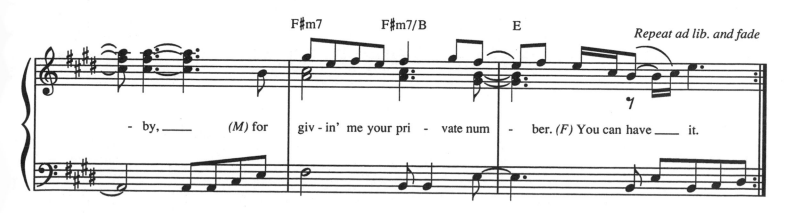

Private Number - 3 - 3

NEEDLES AND PINS

Words and Music by
SONNY BONO and
JACK NITZSCHE

Needles and Pins - 2 - 1

NEVER MY LOVE

Words and Music by
DICK and DON ADDRISI

Moderately

You ask me if there'll come a time when I grow tired of you, Nev-er My Love, Nev-er My Love.

You won-der if this heart of mine will lose its de-sire for you, Nev-er My Love Nev-er My Love.

Never My Love - 2 - 1

OH, PRETTY WOMAN

Words and Music by
ROY ORBISON and
BILL DEES

Oh, Pretty Woman - 4 - 1

ONLY THE LONELY

Words and Music by
ROY ORBISON and
JOE MELSON

Only the Lonely - 2 - 1

- 2 -

ONLY THE LONELY know the heartaches I've been through
ONLY THE LONELY know I cry and cry for you
Maybe tomorrow, a new romance
No more sorrow, but that's the chance
You've got to take if you're lonely
Heartbreak, ONLY THE LONELY

PROUD MARY

Words and Music by
J.C. FOGERTY

RAINDROPS KEEP FALLIN' ON MY HEAD

Words by
HAL DAVID

Music by
BURT BACHARACH

Raindrops Keep Fallin' on My Head - 4 - 1

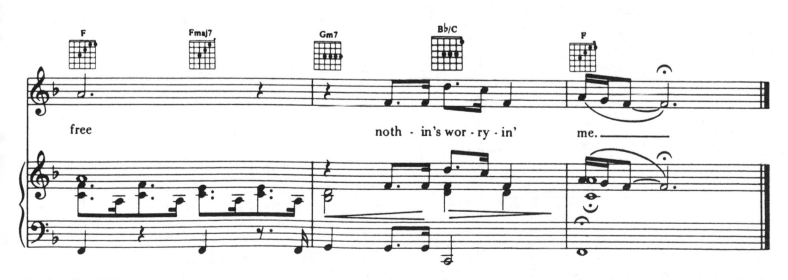

Raindrops Keep Fallin' on My Head - 4 - 4

RESPECT

Words and Music by
OTIS REDDING, JR.

RUNAROUND SUE

Words and Music by
DION DI MUCCI and ERNIE MARESCA

Runaround Sue - 4 - 1

ROSES ARE RED
(My Love)

Words and Music by
AL BYRON and
PAUL EVANS

Roses Are Red - 3 - 1

Roses Are Red - 3 - 2

SOUL MAN

Words and Music by
DAVID PORTER and
ISAAC HAYES

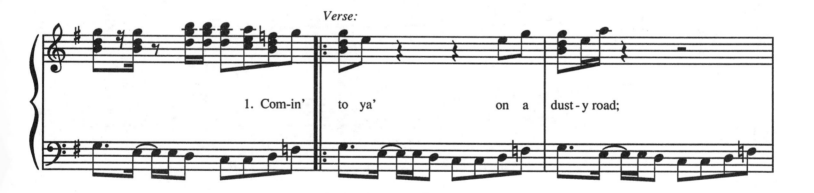

Soul Man - 3 - 1

Verse 2:
Got what I got the hard way,
And I'll make it better each and every day.
So, honey, don't you fret,
'Cause you ain't seen nothin' yet. *(To Chorus:)*

Verse 3:
I was brought up on the south street.
I learned how to love before I could eat.
I was educated at Woodstock.
When I start lovin', oh, I can't stop. *(To Chorus:)*

SEALED WITH A KISS

Words by
PETER UDELL

Music by
GARY GELD

Sealed With a Kiss - 2 - 1

Recorded by BOBBY HEBB on PHILIPS Records

SUNNY

Words and Music by
BOBBY HEBB

Moderate rock

1. Sun - ny, __ yes - ter-day my life was filled with rain. __
2. Sun - ny, __ thank you for the sun - shine __ bou-quet. __

Sun - ny, __ you smiled at me and real - ly eased the pain. __ Oh, the
Sun - ny, __ thank you for the love you've brought my way. __ — You

dark days are done, __ and the bright days are here, __ my sun-ny one __ shines so sin - cere, __ Oh
gave __ to me __ your all __ and all __ Now I feel __ ten feet tall. __

Sun - ny one so true, __ I love you. __

Sunny - 2 - 1

Sunny - 2 - 2

THESE ARMS OF MINE

Words and Music by
OTIS REDDING

The Arms of Mine - 2 - 1

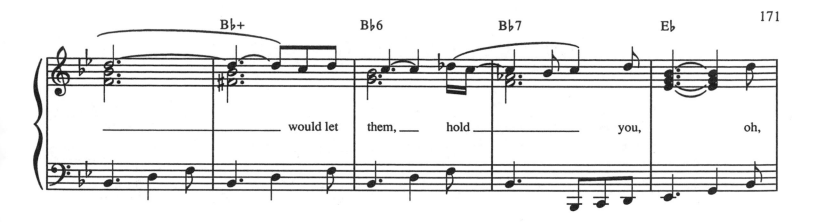

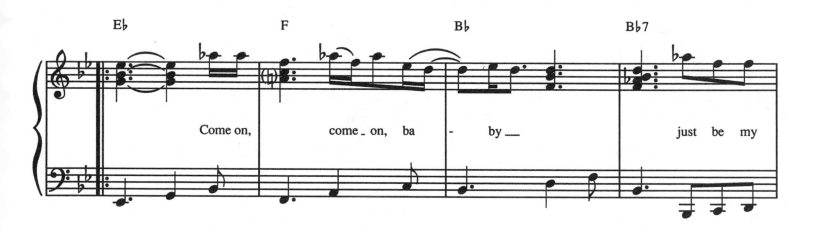

Repeat ad lib. and fade

These Arms of Mine - 2 - 2

THEN YOU CAN TELL ME GOODBYE

Words and Music by
JOHN D. LOUDERMILK

Then You Can Tell Me Goodbye - 3 - 1

TIME OF THE SEASON

By
ROD ARGENT

Moderately Fast

It's the TIME _____ OF THE SEA - SON, when your love runs high.

_____ In this time _____ give it to me ea-sy,

And let me try _____ with pleas-ur'd hands _____ to take you in the

Time of the Season - 3 - 1

sun, To prom-ised lands _____ to show you ev-'ry one. _____ It's the TIME

_____ OF THE SEA - SON for lov - ing. _____

What's your name? _____ Who's your dad-dy?

Is he rich like me? _____ Has he tak - en ___ an - y

TOSSIN' AND TURNIN'

Words and Music by
MALOU RENE and
RITCHIE ADAMS

Ba-by, ba - by can't you see what you're do-ing to me?

With a Beat

I could-n't sleep a wink last night _____ just a-think-ing of

a tempo
mf

you. _____ Ba-by things were-n't right _____ I kept on

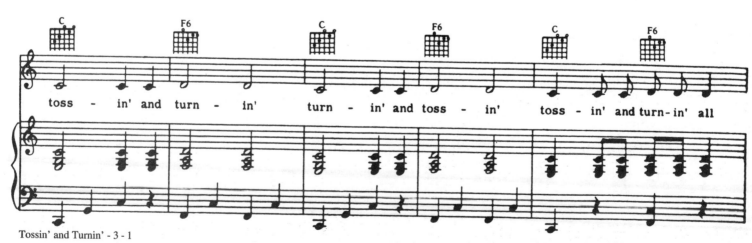

toss - in' and turn - in' turn - in' and toss - in' toss - in' and turn-in' all

Tossin' and Turnin' - 3 - 1

WHEN A MAN LOVES A WOMAN

Words and Music by
CALVIN LEWIS and ANDREW WRIGHT

When a Man Loves a Woman - 3 - 2

TURN! TURN! TURN!
(To Everything There Is A Season)

Words from the
Book of Ecclesiastes

Adaptation and Music by
PETE SEEGER

Turn! Turn! Turn! - 2 - 1

2. A time to build up, a time to break down;
   A time to dance, a time to mourn;
   A time to cast away stones,
   A time to gather stones together.

3. A time of love, a time of hate;
   A time of war, a time of peace;
   A time you may embrace,
   A time to refrain from embracing.

4. A time to gain, a time to lose;
   A time to rend, a time to sew;
   A time to love, a time to hate;
   A time for peace, I swear it's not too late.

Turn! Turn! Turn! - 2 - 2

THE WANDERER

Words and Music by
ERNEST MARESCA

The Wanderer - 2 - 1

The Wanderer - 2 - 2

1. C
2. C
To next strain
round.
2. Well now, there's
round.
Oh well, I
3. C
G7
Fine
round.
roam from town to town,
I go thru
life with - out a care;
And I'm as hap - py as a clown
With my
A7
D7
G7
D. S. al Fine
two fists of i - ron and my bot-tle of beer.
3. Oh well,

WHEN WILL I BE LOVED

Words and Music by
PHIL EVERLY

When Will I Be Loved - 3 - 1

When Will I Be Loved - 3 - 3

A WHITER SHADE OF PALE

Words and Music by
KEITH REID and
GARY BROOKER

In a slow 4

Lyrics:
1. We skipped the light fan - dan - go,
2. She said, "I'm home on shore leave,"
3. She said, "There is no rea - son,

Turned cart - wheels 'cross the floor,
Though in truth we were at sea,
And the truth is plain to see,"

A Whiter Shade of Pale - 3 - 1

Recorded by THE JEFFERSON AIRPLANE

WHITE RABBIT

Words and Music by
GRACE SLICK

Psychedelic Stomp

One pill __ makes you larg-er __ And one pill __ makes you small. And the
you go __ chas-ing rab-bits __ And you know you're __ going to fall. Tell 'em a

ones that __ moth-er gives you don't do an - y - thing at all. Go ask
hoo - kah __ smok-in' cat-er-pil-lar has giv - en you the call. Call

A - lice __ when she's ten feet tall. __ And if
A - lice __ when she was just small. __

When men on the chess-board __ get up and tell you where to go. __ And you've

White Rabbit - 2 - 1

WIPE OUT

By
SURFARIS

Brightly, with a beat

Wipe Out - 2 - 1

WOULDN'T IT BE NICE?

Words by
BRIAN WILSON and
TONY ASHER

Music by
BRIAN WILSON

Would-n't it be nice if we were old - er__ Then__ we would-n't have to wait__ so__
nice if we could wake__ up__ In__ the morn-ing when the day__ is__

long____ And would-n't it be nice to live to - ge - ther In__ the kind of
new____ And af - ter that to spend the day to - ge - ther Hold__ each oth - er

world where we'd__ be - long____ Though it's gon-na make it that much bet - ter__
close the whole__ night__ through__ The hap - py times to-geth - er we'd been spend-ing__

When we can say good-night and stay to - geth - er____ Would-n't it be
I wish that ev - 'ry kiss was nev - er end - ing____

Wouldn't It Be Nice? - 2 - 1

Wouldn't It Be Nice? - 2 - 2

YA YA

Words and Music by
CLARENCE L. LEWIS
and MORRIS LEVY

Ya Ya - 2 - 1

YOU'RE SIXTEEN

Words and Music by
RICHARD M. SHERMAN and
ROBERT B. SHERMAN

You're Sixteen - 3 - 1

From the American Tribal Love-Rock Musical "HAIR"

AQUARIUS/LET THE SUNSHINE IN

Words by
JAMES RADO and GEROME RAGNI

Music by
GALT MacDERMOT

Aquarius/Let the Sunshine In - 5 - 1

Aquarius/Let the Sunshine In - 5 - 3

Aquarius/Let the Sunshine In - 5 - 5

PEPPERMINT TWIST

Words and Music by
JOEY DEE and HENRY GLOVER

Peppermint Twist - 2 - 1

Verse 2

ANGEL BABY

Words and Music by
ROSE HAMLIN

Angel Baby - 4 - 1

Angel Baby - 4 - 4

MONY, MONY

Words and Music by
BOBBY BLOOM, RITCHIE CORDELL,
BO GENTRY and TOMMY JAMES

Mony, Mony - 2 - 1

Mony, Mony - 2 - 2

I THINK WE'RE ALONE NOW

Words and Music by
RITCHIE CORDELL

I Think We're Alone Now - 2 - 1

I Think We're Alone Now - 2 - 2

I LIKE IT LIKE THAT

Words and Music by
CHRIS KENNER

I Like It Like That - 2 - 1

I Like It Like That - 2 - 2

IN-A-GADDA-DA-VIDA

Words and Music by
DOUG INGLE

In-a-gad-da-da-vi - da, hon-ey, don't you know that I love _____ you?_____

In-a-gad-da-da-vi - da, ba - by, don't you know that I'll al - ways be true?_

In-A-Gadda-Da-Vida - 2 - 1

In-A-Gadda-Da-Vida - 2 - 2

ITSY BITSY TEENIE WEENIE
YELLOW POLKA DOT BIKINI

Words and Music by
PAUL J. VANCE and LEE POCKRISS

Itsy Bitsy Teenie Weenie Yellow Polka Dot Bikini - 2 - 1

SPANISH FLEA

Moderately Bright

Music by
JULIUS WECHTER

Spanish Flea - 2 - 1

BIGGEST
POP HITS & COUNTRY HITS
OF 1998

BIGGEST
POP HITS OF 1998

(MF9820) Piano/Vocal/Chords
(AF9835) Easy Piano arr. Coates & Brimhall

- The biggest songs from the hottest artists
- More than 30 hit songs
- Available in P/V/C and Easy Piano Editions

Titles (and artists) include: **I Don't Want to Miss a Thing** (Aerosmith) • **My Heart Will Go On** (Celine Dion) • **How Do I Live** (LeAnn Rimes) • **You're Still the One** (Shania Twain) • **Ray of Light** (Madonna) • **All My Life** (K-Ci & Jo Jo) • **Good Riddance (Time of Your Life)** (Green Day) • **This Kiss** (Faith Hill) • **Kiss the Rain** (Billie Myers) • **Walkin' on the Sun** (Smash Mouth) and many more.

BIGGEST
COUNTRY HITS OF 1998

(MF9819) Piano/Vocal/Chords

- The top country songs of the year
- The hottest country artists
- All of your favorites collected together in one great folio

Titles (and artists) include: **You're Still the One** (Shania Twain) • **This Kiss** (Faith Hill) • **Nothin' But the Taillights** (Clint Black) • **There's Your Trouble** (Dixie Chicks) • **How Do I Live** (LeAnn Rimes) • **From This Moment On** (Shania Twain & Bryan White) • **I Do (Cherish You)** (Mark Wills) • **Cover You in Kisses** (John Michael Montgomery) • **Bad Day to Let You Go** (Bryan White) • **Holes in the Floor of Heaven** (Steve Wariner) and many more.